HOW TO CONQUER A NATION

THE 2014 BEGINNERS GUIDE TO WORLD DOMINATION

MATT BYRON

This is a book of fiction and political satire. It is intended for entertainment purposes only. The author does NOT advocate breaking any laws.

Cover image by: www.psdgraphics.com

MATT**BYRON**.COM

CONTENTS

CHAPTER 1:

PLANNING YOUR VERY FIRST CONQUEST

A NEW HOBBY

You yawn as your friends boast of flying to Mars or poaching endangered species. You're not looking for Ferraris in your driveway or jets on your runway. You want to do something exciting and original. What you crave is your very own nation. It's about time you got one.

THE WORLD IS CALLING

Turn on your television, flip to a major news station – and what do you see? You'll see problems in the world. You'll hear about corrupt governments, economies collapsing and other disasters. This is fantastic news. These countries need your help and leadership. The greater the disaster, the greater the cry for new leadership.

Running your own country isn't like applying for a job at Wal-Mart. The job openings aren't advertised, rather they're seized. When you see chaos in the world, that's where people need you most. Of course, you're not obligated to go where people need you. The better question is: where do you want to rule?

Get a nice territory. Don't settle for craters on the Moon or icebergs in Antarctica. Aim high. Use your Internet browser to open Google Maps. Ignore all the arbitrary "borders" of nations and continents. Europe, Asia and Africa are really just one piece of land – or the "Eastern Continent". North America and South America are one chunk too – the "Western Continent". Antarctica and Australia are two tiny islands, which experienced dictators refer to as "Dinghy One" and "Dinghy Two" respectively. Under this new paradigm the world is simple. It's just two peaceful continents and some dinghies floating in a puddle. Now that you've mastered geography, how would you like to divide and conquer the world?

Do some introspective soul searching. Choosing the right country to conquer is a very personal choice. Do you want to rule a billion people or a mere 100 million? Do you want vast fields of oil or expansive wilderness filled with grizzly bears, lost hipsters and moonshine distilleries? Do you want a digital economy or one negotiated in Spanish doubloons?

While reflecting on your options, consider how

much chaos you would like. If you build a new nation from scratch, you'll have modern infrastructure, a clear legal system and few problems. But if you conquer an established nation, you'll have a hodgepodge of legal, social, health, and resource challenges.

Don't over think things though. Reassure yourself that there are thousands of politicians who don't put any thought into their actions. They don't lose sleep over altruistic goals. They rule mainly for the perks that come with the job: a cushy pension, immunity from speeding tickets and the ability to rationalize romantic affairs.

Print out a map of the world. Then use a red crayon to circle your ideal territory and post it on your bedroom wall. If you haven't decided yet, then hurl a dart at the map to choose a location. Remember, if you don't like the country that you conquer, you can return it within 30 days for a full refund (keep your receipts).

The territory you claim will hereinafter be

codenamed "Bestland". But you can call it anything you want.

TESTING THE WATERS

New dictators often ask: "Shouldn't I start small and test the waters?"

No.

If you wanted to start small you could have bought an island on PrivateIslandsOnline.com. But now it's too late. You hold this book in your hand – like a winning lottery ticket. Now you just need to cash it in.

Ruling a nation is your destiny. You cannot escape this fate. Embrace the burden of riches.

WHAT'S YOUR STYLE?

How shall you reign? Your main options are: puppet-master, royalty, elected official and dictator.

PUPPET-MASTER

These are people behind the scenes who call the shots. They secretly run nations and place officials into public offices. They are understated leaders of great power. If you want to learn how to become a puppet master – watch *Godfather I* and *Godfather II*. The downfall of being a puppet-master is the lack of recognition.

ROYALTY

This means you inherited your job. You received your title by mere luck rather than merit. Most modern royal families built their riches through colonialism, where they enslaved the poor and looted the natural resources of developing nations. There can be no worse stigma than the title of royalty. Royalty is passé and demonstrates a lack of ambition. It's for the leaches of society.

ELECTED OFFICIAL

This means you're an idealist. While your desire to run a country is built on the premise that the incumbent government isn't working – you still believe in democracy. Democracies are ineffective because the politicians are always preoccupied with the next election, rather than leading.

Winning democratic elections requires two key things: the support of the people and money. The best way to gain the most support of the masses is by demagoguery and making false promises. Politicians who win the popular vote are the ones who lie the most. Secondly, campaigns rely upon "fundraising" or bribes from lobbyists. Accepting bribes clouds judgment.

Although the democratic process is built on lies and bribes, it might appeal to you for those very reasons

(This book was not written to judge your values or lack of values). So… how can you win a campaign?

First, disregard important issues like the economy, healthcare, national debt and wars. Only 2% of your constituents are political junkies who research the issues. While they represent just 2% of the voting public they will create 90% of your headaches. They will research your candidacy rigorously, critique your opinions, and waste your time caviling.

Most people don't care about politics. The general population spends their time on better things like working, raising a family, playing video games, watching basketball on television and drinking beer. They will never research your campaign. Rather, they will make their decisions based on: if you're physically attractive, you have a nice smile, who your spouse is, and if you have pets. Does owning a dog make you better qualified to run for office? Of course not. But if you have a dog and voters love dogs, then the voters will love you.

Winning a political election is no different than a high school popularity contest. If people like you as a person then you will win. Being likable is all that matters. Don't worry about the issues.

DICTATORS

Alas, the best type of leader is the dictator. These are honest people who lead with a singular focus and uncompromising vision.

If your citizens ask, "Do we look fat?" you can reply without hesitation "Yes 35% of you are obese and we're going to do something about it. I'm grounding everyone until you get in shape." (Conversely, an elected official might not want to stop obesity. An elected official's interests might be convoluted by a major health insurance lobby.) As a dictator you can be honest and get things done.

Dictators don't waste time on elections or appeasing lobbyists. They rule without the need for market surveys and focus groups. Dictators don't need steering committees to convolute decisions, or "fact" finding studies based on biased data. Yes, there is generally a stigma towards dictators, but you can be the first dictator to change that.

To become a dictator you must overthrow an incumbent or incumbents (hopefully you are planning to conquer several countries). By virtue of this ousting process you will demonstrate your ability to effectively lead.

After considering the pros and cons of being a puppet-master, royalty, or elected official – the benefit of being a dictator should be clear. It gives you the most unobstructed path to ruling a nation and unlimited power.

YOUR TEAM

Earlier, you used a red crayon to mark your new turf. Now it's time to turn that goal into a reality.

Before you seize power, you need to have the right team in place. To run the most powerful regime, you should hire the very best people. Throughout the world there are thousands of incompetent politicians. The only reason these counties have not toppled is because talented professionals are constantly undoing the politician's mistakes. Even if you're brilliant, you should surround yourself with the very best people. There are two key teams you will need to assemble: your media gurus and your military.

MEDIA

Ruling a nation requires that people are constantly reminded of your presence. It's vital that your followers are reminded daily that you protect them from evil. If your subjects don't hear about you in the news, they will forget you are in power. Your media network will assure that you look good and are publically visible at all times. They will also facilitate cover-ups and create propaganda films as needed. However, to maintain maximum effectiveness, it is important that your media team appear unaffiliated. Every once in a while they might even cover a bad story on you, just to affirm this impartial image. For example, they might criticize you for not wearing sun block on a sunny day and call your behavior reckless.

Recruit film students for your media team. Promise them ownership of the movie theaters in the nation you conquer.

MILITARY

Dictators need muscle to maintain their power. Right now your power might be limited to an old water gun and some plastic toy soldiers – this is okay. Do you really think someone a thousand miles away is going to audit your military force? Of course not. They will size-up your military based on what they see on television and on the Internet – all of which can be easily faked by using stock video footage and photo editing software. From now on the truth will be whatever you project it to be.

When you start your own militia, you're likely to be labeled a "terrorist". When this happens, just remind people that Benjamin Franklin, George Washington and Thomas Jefferson – America's Founding Fathers – were all considered terrorists by the British. Yet those terrorists now have their faces on America's currency.

How can you recruit people without any money? Where can you find rebels without a cause? Look no further than your local high school or college career fair. It shouldn't be hard to find young people there who are idealistic and energetic. These people want to make the world a better place. They just need a cause to fight for, a direction in which to steer their energy. You could call your program an "internship" so they won't question working without pay. Call it a "grassroots movement" while portraying yourself as the underdog in David vs. Goliath. Make them feel as if they are part of a movement against "the man", "the system" or "the rich".

As you build your army of interns, develop a leadership pyramid. Create titles like "General" or "Chief", for your team. Allow your most seasoned and most loyal to manage platoons of other interns. Giving your troops formal sounding titles and people to manage will fuel their egos and make them feel important. If they press you for payment, promise them land in the territory that you conquer. This will give them a vested interest in the success of your operation.

There is one more group of people you can easily recruit – starving actors. They will act as soldiers in your films. Ironically, their performance in films will have a bigger impact than soldiers in real battles.

Your military only needs about 100 people. All of their work will be staged on propaganda films. With 100 troops (interns and actors combined), green-screen technology, and a creative media team, you'll be able to fake anything.

The perception of reality is more important than reality. The truth will be whatever you project on film.

BUYING YOUR NATION

Now you might be thinking, "How do I buy a land for my nation?" or "Can I use my credit card to buy it?" These are common concerns for any first time ruler. You can publically buy land, as the United States bought Alaska from Russia in 1867, but that option is too historically accurate to be helpful. A better use of your money is a good bribe… so it's time to get some gold.

Owning real gold is cost prohibitive. So you may need to hire a good alchemist or experienced counterfeiter. Search your local phonebook or the Internet for one of these reputable professionals. Check their references and reviews on Google.

Once you meet with your alchemist or counterfeiter, order 400-troy-ounce bars (this is the standard size used by central banks) of tungsten. Get the bars stamped ".999 pure gold" and spray painted a gold color. Tungsten is cheap and has almost the same density as gold.

Gold bars are the currency of choice for any corrupt world leader. Your goal is not to buy a country for the full market price – that would require trillions in gold. Rather, your goal is to bribe the incumbent ruler. A single bar of gold will be worth anywhere from $500,000 to $1 million depending on the commodities markets. Don't worry about the exact value. All that matters is that gold is worth a lot of money and it's hard to trace. Show any politician 50 bars of gold, and he/she will give you the keys to the country. That's your goal. Just a quick bribe.

There are two simple things you can do to make the counterfeit gold appear real. First, you should present the gold in aluminum Halliburton suitcases. You might even handcuff these to your wrists – this really adds to the presentation. Second, you should not be surprised if the politician asks for a certificate of authenticity. Print one of these *prior* to making the bribe. A typical certificate of authenticity will read something to the effect of "This gold is definitely real. Don't dent, puncture or melt this bar because then it will be less collectible." As a final touch, add a holographic sticker to the certificate of authenticity. A holographic pirate skull or star will suffice. Holograms can easily be found at Wal-Mart or your local counterfeiting center. Attention to these formal nuances will make the purity of your gold irrefutable.

CHAPTER 2:

YOUR COUP D'ÉTAT

TIME TO CONQUER

Naturally, you're exited about your first coup. You're likely counting your empty bottles of wine to determine how many Molotov cocktails you can make. But hold on just a second, violent coups are risky.

In this day and age, wars are won in the media, not on the battlefield. To win a war you need only project the illusion of having fought and won. If an actual war is never reported to the public, then it's as if the war never happened. How many unreported wars have impacted your life? Conversely, if a fictitious war is reported as real, then it will impact people's lives. This was proven by the 1938 radio broadcast of *War of the Worlds*. Many listeners panicked as they heard about the alien invasion. They had a very real reaction to the fictitious event. Therefore, reality is whatever you project it to be.

Your war will be won by producing a series of

short films. Remember, not only is an actual battle likely to land you in jail or get you injured or killed; but more importantly, you can lose a real battle.

Direct your media team to create the following short films to highlight your rise to power. (None of these films should be released until they are all produced. Then these films can be leaked out one at a time or simultaneously.)

The Evil Government: the first film must build the support of the people you're going to conquer. You want them to know you have a heart (this may or may not be the case) and good intentions (this may or may not be the case). This film portrays the incumbent government ruining people's lives, overtaxing them and restricting their freedom.

The Rise of the Hero: This builds upon the premise that the government has been suppressing the people. This film portrays you as an average citizen who has been wronged by the government. Perhaps the government gave you a parking ticket or is holding your dog hostage. In this film, you do what any normal citizen would do, you rise up.

Fall of the Empire: In this film your personal struggle against the government is joined by thousands of volunteers. This is where your army of actors, green-screen editing, and media team will really need to shine. Film your actors fighting in front of green-screens. Then direct your media team to superimpose those fights over video footage of the capital city.

Don't release the films yet. First you must meet with the incumbent ruler. To arrange this meeting call his/her office and indicate that you are a business investor interested in making a "campaign donation". No politician will ever turn down a chance to meet with a "donor".

Bring your two Halliburton suitcases of gold to this meeting. Also bring your militia actors dressed in camouflage. (This will add to the illusion of your force and make your offer more compelling.)

When you meet with the incumbent leader tell him/her "I'll offer you fifty gold bars to leave this city and declare me the leader. If you do not leave right now, my militia will kill you."

When faced with the choice of riches or death, any wise dictator will take the gold and run. If that doesn't work then resort to blackmail. The people of Bestland do not need to know their former leader was bribed or blackmailed. That would go over poorly with the public. Let the people of Bestland believe the stories portrayed in your films.

Now that the old regime has left, it's time for the finishing touches to seal the legitimacy of the new regime. It's time to produce one last film: *The Cover-up*. It's a film where the old government regime is portrayed as trying to cover-up the coup and first three films. This is important, because it explains why the local citizens of the capital city were not aware of the takeover. Feed this forth film to conspiracy theorists. They will find real life evidence that supports the validity of the coup.

You've now seized power without real money or actual violence. Your extensive planning has paid off. Congratulations.

CHAPTER 3:
ADMIN

LOOKING OFFICIAL

You've seized power, but now you need to maintain it. Therefore you must project an illusion of power. The more powerful you appear, the less likely you'll be challenged.

For men this means wearing a suit, cufflinks, gold tassels on your shoulders, medals pinned to your chest and a necklace made of polished bullet casings. A similar dress code should be adopted by female dictators. The top members from your coup will need proper uniforms too. Take care of these men and women, because they helped you get into office. They are the ones you can trust the most, so keep them well bribed with vast swaths of land.

Your image and power must be conveyed in how you travel. If the President of the United States arrived at your door riding a skateboard and tattered clothes would you take him seriously? Of course not. But if the President arrives in an armored caravan of fifty vehicles and wears a suit – then you might will perceive him differently. Power is an illusion. Master it.

Start with an entourage of five black SUVs with tinted windows. Get these vehicles outfitted with police lights. Travel with 10-20 members of your military at all times. They should wear bulletproof vests, ear pieces and sunglasses. It doesn't matter if they're listening to music in their ear pieces. What matters is that these dudes look serious.

You look official and travel in style. Now it's time to run your nation.

LAWS

Some countries have hundreds if not thousands of laws. The more laws you have, the more diluted and ineffective they become. If you keep your legal system simple, people will understand the laws. If you make your legal system convoluted your citizens will constantly break them. Therefore, by having many laws you can legally arrest any citizen at any time. Two laws are highly recommended to all dictators:

1. Any attempt to overthrow the Dictator will be considered an act of treason and punishable by death". (This law helps you keep your job and stay alive.)

2. All transaction must be conducted in the local currency. All taxes must be paid using the local currency. (You need to control the monetary system to control the people.)

THE JOY OF TAXES

Gone are the days of paying taxes, now you get to receive them. Did you ever think you would love taxes? Did you ever think you would get paid to suppress people?

Taxes are the glue that keeps a nation together. By requiring citizens to pay taxes (with your currency) you create a demand for your currency. If you don't tax your citizens they could use a different currency. A nation will fall apart without a tax system. Taxation keeps the government strong and the citizens weak.

You must tax your citizens, even if it's just .0001 % per year.

YOUR FIRST CURRENCY

Your government must have a currency system to maintain power. Printing your own money allows you to fund vital projects like schools, your military and your private Boeing 747 aircraft.

Put a picture of yourself on your currency. This will remind citizens of their dictator. Think of yourself as a brand - like Nike or Microsoft. The more people see your picture or your logo, the more they'll think of you. Additional features on your currency can be historical sites, your nation's motto, and social messages.

Effective anti-counterfeiting measures include smiley face watermarks, security threads and glitter ink. For watermarks and other supplies, search Google for vendors. If anyone counterfeits your money, punish them by death or offer them employment at your bureau of engraving and printing.

If anyone ever asks, "What backs your currency?" Tell them it's backed by, "100 tons of gold bars hidden in a secret vault." You might be pressed further when they ask, "Where is it?" To which should respond, "It's in a secret location obviously."

Nations that actually have gold will never disclose the location (due to security concerns). Any nation which reveals the location of its gold bars obviously doesn't have any.

If you ever want to destroy another nation, undermine its taxation system and currency. *Make a note of this for your future expansion.*

NAMING YOUR COUNTRY & RECOGNITION

Here are a couple of quick tips for formally announcing your new regime to the world:

1. Create a catchy name for your country. Keep in mind the name will affect how people perceive your territory. A name like "Bestland" or "Hell on Earth" will likely be received better than a name like "Iceland".

2. Issue a press release or Tweet, declaring the establishment of your country.

3. Contact cartographers and recommend they update their maps to show Bestland.

Cartographers love political turmoil for this reason. If maps weren't changing annually, they might starve.

4. Update your occupation on LinkedIn.com to "Dictator". Then connect with other dictators throughout the world.

5. Order a brass nametag for your desk to read "Dictator". Engraving anything in stone or metal will give it more credibility.

6. Hire programming gurus to build a website for your new nation. Get the URL to end in ".gov" so it looks official. If you can't get ".gov" then buy a URL ending in ".org".

7. Update your Facebook status to "juggernaut."

PATRIOTISM

Your citizens need a cultural identity to rationalize traditions. Think of the United States. There, people proudly speak of America declaring its independence from the British in 1776. Over 200 years have passed, nobody alive experienced this event first-hand, yet they proudly boast of this history. Is it true or not? It might be. It might not be. Who's to say that it wasn't in the year 1777 or 1677? Who knows if the event even happened? If two opposing news stations can distort the news occurring today, then how distorted do you think "facts" become over centuries? It is for this very reason you can completely fabricate your nation's history and traditions.

Without a cultural identity your people will feel lost. But with it, your nation will develop strong patriotic roots. Patriotism will unite your nation and keep you in power.

You can't control the present or the future, but you can alter how history was recorded (especially in the digital age). As the leader of Bestland, you will want many stories. The more patriotic stories you fabricate, the more established your nation will sound. If you're going to lie, do so boldly. Consider this example:

> *According to the 1750 census, there were 25,683,079.1 citizens of Bestland. In 1751 the Emperor of Mountainland attacked the peaceful people in Bestland. During the invasion many Bestlanders fled, since they had no weapons. The Mountainland armies killed 2,500,100 Bestlanders. To this day, many of our citizens are still hiding in foreign countries. They fear political prosecution. So although only 105 citizens are prominent at this time – millions more are still in hiding. Under my leadership, I will free the millions of my citizens who are suppressed. I am doing this to honor our ancestors and for the benefit of the children of tomorrow.*

Not only does this believable fib establish your nation as having many citizens, but it also sets the stage for future expansion. Then you can follow it with a statement like this:

Today, Bestland bombed Mountainland. We did not wish to go to war. But Mountainland ignored our two formal text messaged warnings. Therefore, we will now occupy Mountainland until all of our suppressed citizens are free.

Notice how the unprovoked war was spun into a humanitarian mission. *More on euphemisms later.*

To further promote patriotism you should create holidays. People love getting paid time off from work – regardless of the reason. Commemorate your political coup, the invention of the wheel, or bottled water.

CITIZENS WANT TO KNOW THEIR LEADER

Just as it is important to fabricate your nation's history, it's equally important to fabricate your personal history. Your followers will want to know about your past. School children will want to know what you were like as a kid – they'll want to know your favorite sports, cartoons and pranks. College students will want to know about your major, your GPA and how you managed to graduate. Adults will want to know about your professional qualifications, how you became the great leader you now purport to be and what your vision is for the future. To please all these people, you'll want to have a minimum of the following:

Autobiography: Don't sweat it, most famous people don't write their own books. When they lie about authoring a book it's not called "plagiarism," it's called "hiring a ghost writer."

Independent movie: For those who are too lazy to read, the movie is the genre of choice. Instruct your media team to produce this film without an official endorsement by you. Get it labeled "an independent film." This way it will appear impartial and bold. As a general rule, people will think you're bragging if you talk about yourself. Thus it is important to secretly pay others to boast about you. (It's okay to manipulate people as long as it's for a good cause.) This film is a great opportunity for releasing some long lost/fabricated pictures. Like one from your childhood where you're protesting war, a picture from your college days when you helped save people from the rubble of an earthquake and the picture of you carving a turkey for the troops during the holidays.

Holidays: If you propose a holiday in your own name it will sound conceited. But if the idea is proposed by a third party, it will sound like genuine praise. Therefore instruct your media team to fabricate a letter - maybe from a group of school children or an elderly widow – which proposes a holiday in your name. Let your citizens celebrate your greatness at least once per year.

GRANDSTANDING

Anytime there is a natural disaster or tragedy, leverage the opportunity to speak to your people. Your speech should do a couple things: explain the event, mourn the loss, state the government has everything under control and thank God.

For example, if a massive glacier cuts through your capital city you could say:

Our nation suffered a great loss today, as a melting glacier crushed nearly 20 homes and businesses. It killed two sunflowers and three dogs. Our government will rebuild those homes and businesses in the times ahead, but our government cannot rebuild those two sunflowers and three dogs. May we learn from this experience and move forward with great resolve. Our hearts and prayers go out to the victims, their friends, their families and pet owners worldwide. May God bless you and Bestland. Thank you.

Every crisis is an opportunity to reaffirm your value as a leader and the role of government to the people. Never let a good crisis go to waste.

YOUR GRANDIOSE VISION

Egyptian leaders built pyramids, President Eisenhower gave America highways, and President Kennedy put some guys on the Moon.

Great leaders inspire their people to undertake massive projects. Your vision need not be economical or logical. Quite the contrary. The more ridiculous, wasteful and quixotic – the better. Massive public projects create jobs, and employed people are a happy people. Conversely, unemployed people stage insurrections.

Your followers will think "Dictator ________ (insert your name here) brought us the ________ (insert project name: stairway to the sun, tunnel to the center of the earth, giant meteor-catching baseball glove, etc.)." This project will boost nationalism and serve as a physical manifestation of the power wielded by your regime.

Perhaps most importantly this project will instill fear in your enemies. Other nations planning to attack your regime will pause to reflect. They will say "Dictator ____________ (insert your name here) built the ____________ (insert project name: weather machine, second moon, robotic dragon etc.). Clearly, this dictator is insane and his/her nation is a prosperous one. Who else could afford such a wasteful project?"

As an added benefit, if your project is insane then other world leaders will assume you're insane. Insane leaders are impossible to predict and therefore dangerous. If you appear insane, other world leaders will consider you extremely dangerous. They will be less likely to attack.

Dream boldly. Be ridiculous. If you need help, ask a committee of five-year-olds for ideas. Children speak their mind and don't care about money. They are the perfect advisors for the massive project which will consume 90% of your nation's resources, after all they're also the ones who will live with the consequences.

Not only are children great advisors, but they can also be used to rationalize anything. If anyone asks why you're building this project, explain "It's not for you, it's not for me, it's for the children of posterity." Helping the children of tomorrow is a cause that few people can rebut.

GIVE THEM ELECTIONS

As a dictator it may be wise to give your citizens elections. If you do, your citizens won't complain about a lack of choice. The *appearance* of legitimate elections will help prevent a violent insurrection.

Finance and support weak candidates to run against yourself. Then once they win the primaries, crush them in the general election or make them "disappear".

Delay results until *after* the polls close (this gives the illusion the ballots were counted) and makes it appear like a close election.

WAR

Your citizens need heroes. Naturally, you will be known as the hero who helped them overthrow the previous tyrannical regime. But you're just one person. Your citizens need heroes in their everyday lives. How can you fill your nation with heroes? Go to war.

Send your troops on bogus missions to blow up mountains. Direct them to blowup hidden bunkers which hide weapons of mass destruction. Or if that sounds too risky, instruct your troops to fly remote controlled drones over foreign lands. By using robots to kill people, you will avoid any casualties. If you don't want to hurt anyone, instruct your troops to play a video game where they think they are flying drones. Wars are great team-building exercises for nations. They unite the citizens, create heroes and untimely boost patriotism.

SUCCESS

How can you measure the success of your regime?

1) By the number of times your nation is searched on Google

2) By the number of “likes” people have given you on Facebook

3) By the number of countries you conquer

4) By the number of subscribers on your YouTube channel

REDIRECTING THE ANGER AND DISAPPOINTMENT

It is impossible to please all of your constituents. So how can you deflect hatred? Use scapegoats. Consider this example:

Problem: Your followers are angry at you for crashing the economy.

Solution: Redirect that anger towards some other country – preferably one on the opposite side of the world. Blame that country for unfairly making goods too affordable. If that doesn't work, blame the rich. Blame the top 1% of the wealthy people in your nation for causing the economic crisis. Remember, it's the rich people who create poor people. If you didn't have rich people, you wouldn't have the contrast necessary to identify the poor.

By giving your constituents an outlet for their anger, they are less likely to assassinate you.

KEEP YOUR PEOPLE IN FEAR

The most effective way to keep people under your control is by keeping them in fear. This will prevent them from ousting you. Keeping your people in fear will make them grateful that you suppress them. This is most easily accomplished by using fake problems.

How do fake problems work? It's simple. Direct your media team to cover the story of a fictitious avian flu or bearded terrorist group. After 60-90 days, when the hype borders on hysteria, announce that you've solved the problem. Announce the terrorists have been killed or the disease eradicated. Or if you want a more interesting story, announce that the bird flu killed the terrorists.

Solving fake problems will build your credibility as a leader. Most citizens assume their leaders are incompetent. So when you solve problems, your people will be shocked. They will immediately have a greater respect for your leadership. The beauty of fake problems – like terrorists and bird flues – is that few people will ever have the interest or financial means to determine if they actually exist. In the case of the assassinated terrorist, claim the body was dumped into the ocean. In the case of the disease – claim it's eradicated and safely contained in a lab on Plum Island. Case closed.

Perhaps the best fake problem is that of foreign invasion. Instruct your media team to broadcast stories about the hostile intentions of a nation 8,000 miles away. Xenophobia spreads quickly, especially when there's a massive geographic divide. The less people understand something, the more they will fear it. When your citizens fear a foreign invasion, they will look to the government for protection. The idea of an invasion may be logistically impossible, but most of your citizens won't realize that.

If your media team inundates the television with

stories of terror daily, then these ideas will become dogmatic in your citizens' minds. For maximum effectiveness, develop a color coated danger warning system. The warning should range from a "high alert" or the color red to "low" or the color green. If you try to keep your citizens in a high level of fear at all times, they will become acclimated to your system. It will become ineffective. Therefore, to keep your citizens sensitive and responsive to this fear gauge make the threat level arbitrarily oscillate.

While your citizens are distracted by fake problems, you'll be able to gloss over the real problems. These may include the fact that paper money is worthless, LIBOR is corrupt, your nation depends on foreign energy, or that you're unqualified to lead.

Fake problems and real problems will terrify your people. Give your subjects hope by solving fake problems and prevent chaos by shielding them from real problems.

It's okay to deceive your citizens as long as it creates stability.

SOUND-BITES ARE YOUR FRIEND

Logical statements are well substantiated in context. But when you take a sound-bite out of context, it can be construed anyway you like. Suppose your political foe says "War is not the answer." You can ask your media team to omit the word "not" from this statement and quote your nemesis as saying "War is… the answer."

Such tactics are par for the course. You should expect your opponents to employ them..

PHOTO OPPORTUNITIES

Never miss a good photo opportunity. Why are photos important? Anytime a constituent has a photo taken with the leader of his/her nation, the photo will be framed, posted on his/her Facebook, and shown to a thousand people. Not only will it make the constituent feel important but it will also boost your public image.

ALLITERATIONS, CLICHÉS, EUPHEMISMS AND RHYMES

As a ruler you must be tactful. Alliterations, clichés, euphemisms and rhymes, are some of the best tools for dodging political disasters.

Here are some of the best lines of all time and explanations of their genius:

Too big to fail: Draws a sacrosanct conclusion without a logical premise.

Fighting for peace: Rationalizes any war as a humanitarian cause.

Numbers don't lie: Overlooks the fact that the people who produce them lie and that equations (like Gross Domestic Product and Unemployment) are often manipulated or "revised".

If you're not with us then you're against us: Forces people to take sides on an issue, even though they do not have any reason to be involved.

Your vote is important: As long as voters think they have a voice, they will be less likely to seek political office. This acquiesces constituents and deters them from running against you for office.

History repeats itself: Yes the sun is likely to rise

and fall, but everything else is bound to change. This one is great for rationalizing the irrational.

A million people can't be wrong: Incorrectly assumes that a single one of them is thinking.

The children are our future: Rationalizes making real sacrifices today for people that do not yet exist.

Use the aforementioned statements to dodge political bullets.

PANDERING

Elected politicians pander – which is a sign of weakness. They do this to appease the masses, but in doing so lie extensively.

How can you still maintain the support of your people without pandering? The answer is simple: answer all questions with questions. Consider this common situation:

Constituent: Do you want to raise or lower taxes?

You: Why don't you mind your own business?

Constituent: What do you mean?

You: Who is your ruler?

Constituent: You are.

You: Do trust me?

Constituent: Not really.

You: Then why do you care what I say? If you don't trust me then it doesn't matter what I say, isn't that right? If you're asking a question then clearly you care about my opinion and therefore you trust me.

Constituent: Well I guess that's true. I never thought of that.

You: So you trust me?

Constituent: Yes.

You: As your dictator do you think I want a strong nation or a weak one?

Constituent: Well gee, I never thought of that. A strong one right?

You: Yes, of course. And as your dictator, how do you think I keep our nation strong?

Constituent: By keeping the people happy and prosperous.

You: Yes. Exactly. Now what is your job, my dear constituent?

Constituent. I am a baker.

You: Now go forth and bake bread. Make the finest bread in all the world. Keep our people fed, so our nation will stay strong. The strength of our nation depends on people like you. You make a difference.

Constituent: Yes. Thank you for your ruling over us. I am so grateful to have such a kind and wise ruler suppressing me. Thank you for answering my question and empowering me.

Now, it's unlikely you'll experience the exact example above. But what is more important, is that through your rejoinder:

1) You have taken control of the conversation by asking questions. As a dictator you must always maintain control.

2) You explained to your constituent that you both share a common vested interest in the well being of your nation. Not only does this create comradery, but it also builds trust. Your interests are aligned. So it makes the constituent believe

your intentions.

3) Your blandishments have reminded your constituent that he has a value in society – that of a baker. The occupation of the constituent could be replaced with anything, from brain surgeon to street sweeper. In truth, all of your people add value to your society. Therefore all people should be genuinely appreciated. Even criminals add value, they create jobs for law enforcement officers. But what is most important, is that you made your constituent feel special. People like to feel appreciated.

4) The closing remarks from the above example made the constituent feel empowered to make a difference. You reminded him that his

contribution to society is an important one – this is true. You reminded him that a nation is not just a piece of land. It is the actions of the individuals that make the nation great.

You have turned an insolent constituent into one of your followers. Prior to the conversation there was 1 person who hated you, now there is 1 who loves you. That means a net score increase of +2. This is good. Think of your constituents as numbers, otherwise you might develop a conscious.

Your nation will always have problems. You will never have enough time and resources to address these problems on your own. Rather than allowing people to pawn off problems onto your shoulders, put the onerous challenges back on them. Make them feel important and empowered. Make them feel like the instruments of change in your nation. They can change your country for the better or for worse – your statements are not entirely patronizing. Pandering will dissolve a nation, questioning citizens will unite it.

If all else fails, ask a question which redirects the focus towards the children of posterity. Anyone trying to overcome that rebuttal will quickly be called a "Scrooge."

Consider these examples:

Constituent: Why are we at war?

You: We are at war to create peace for the children of tomorrow. Do you think it is better we fight or that the children die?

Constituent: How can you possibly cut social welfare programs for the elderly?

You: Would you rather children starve?

Constituent: How can you raise taxes?

You: Would you rather close children's schools?

Answer questions with questions. Avoid the problems of today by focusing on the children of tomorrow. Your responses need not be logical. The objective is to put the blame on your constituents and make them feel ashamed.

CHAPTER 4:

BENEVOLENT DICTATOR ASSESSMENT TEST

At this point you're already ruling a nation. Maybe you've run it into the ground or maybe you've created a utopia. Either way it never hurts to build your political resume. The Benevolent Dictator Assessment Test (BDAT) may help you gain greater professional prestige.

This test was designed by major world leaders to assess the potential of new dictators. A high score on this test will give you street credit in the most elite circles of world dictators.

BENEVOLENT DICTATOR ASSESSMENT TEST

1. Which nation is best?

A) Your nation

B) The nation with the highest Gross Domestic Product

C) The most prosperous nation with the most smiling citizens

D) The Roman Empire before it fell

2. How can you avoid pandering?

A) By telling people the truth

B) By answering questions with questions and encouraging your citizens to be the agents of change

C) By being a dictator

D) All of the above

3. Why do you want to implement the new $100 trillion __________ (insert any name) program?

A) It offers a 300 % rate of return on your investment

B) To save the environment

C) To trick other nations into thinking that your nation is prosperous and convince them you are insane

D) To protect world peace

4. Who should be a dictator?

A) You

B) You

C) You

D) All of the above

5. If you are called a terrorist what should you do?

A) Punch the accuser in the face

B) Offer the accuser a job on your staff.

C) Tell the accuser that movies are making him/her paranoid

D) All of the above

6. Why should your country go to war?

A) To expand your territory

B) To stand for justice in the face of an unspeakable evil

C) To build nationalism and create jobs

D) To fight boredom

7. What is the best way to win a war?

A) To not have one

B) By incurring the fewest casualties

C) By instructing your media team to fabricate everything from the newspaper stories to field report videos

8. A tractor trailer truck on a one lane road gets stuck under an overpass. The vehicle is now blocking the road. The roof of the truck is 1 inch too tall to clear the overpass. The truck is mechanically sound but the vehicle is wedged under the bridge. The driver is bewildered and needs advice. Your armored convoy of 5 SUVs and 15 guards are the first to arrive on the scene. Which of the following to you do:

A) Direct your team of guards to push the truck out.

B) Call for a helicopter so you can continue onto your destination.

C) Direct your security team to prepare for an ambush by securing the perimeter. Once the area is secured, then instruct the truck driver to release some air out of the tires. This will lower the height of the truck and allow it to clear the overpass. Once the problem is solved pose for a photo opportunity with your constituent. Then forward this photo to your press team, so they may acclaim your deed.

9. Bestland's urban areas suffer from an obesity epidemic and rising food prices. What do you do?

A) Allow food prices to rise until people starve. This will force your citizens to lose weight and thereby end obesity.

B) Encourage your citizens to plant thousands of fruit trees in city parks and along the sidewalks. Point out that healthy foods (i.e. rice and beans) are cheaper per pound than fast food. Recommend that your citizens eat healthily and exercise, because a nation can only be strong if its people are healthy.

C) Ban the consumption of bacon.

10. Bestland imports 10 million barrels of oil per day from the country of Oilland. Although Oilland is a peaceful nation, they have decided to stop exporting oil because prices are too low. The lack of oil will paralyze your economy overnight. How should you nation react?

A) Undermine the currency of Oilland by forcing their citizens to use Bestland's currency.

B) Attack Oilland under the guise a humanitarian mission.

C) Distract your citizens with your cute new dog.

D) All of the above.

BDAT ANSWER KEY

How did you do on the BDAT? You rocked it obviously. If your answers differ from the answer key, then the answer key was wrong. As a dictator you are always right. But just in case you're curious, below you will find the answers given by leading politicians:

1. A) Your nation is the best. Never admit that any other nation is greater than yours.

2. D) All of the above. Pandering is a sign of weakness which is often used by elected officials. As a dictator you can be honest since you do not accept bribes or worry about elections.

3. C) By wasting resources other nations will assume Bestland is prosperous and powerful. Projecting strength to the world will prevent other nations from attacking Bestland.

4. There is no wrong answer to this question. This question was designed to make you feel like a voter looking at a ballot. You felt like you had a choice although you really didn't. As a dictator you can use mind games like this to make your voters feel like they actually have a choice in their elections.

5. B) Hire the person. If you are surrounded by "yes-men" you will become disconnected. It's good to have some honest people around you.

6. C) The greatest benefit of war is that it creates nationalism which unites your citizens. Blowing-up stuff also creates jobs. Gaining territory and fighting evil are cute goals, but really just a distraction from what is most important – that you keep your nation unified and prosperous.

7. C) The best way to win wars is by faking them on video. Your citizens will never have the resources to audit your stories. As long as your videos are professionally produced, you should be able to project any "reality" you wish. Reality is whatever you project it to be on film.

8. C) While your guards might be able to push the vehicle out, this would leave you unguarded. Therefore it is too great a security risk. You could

fly off to your destination by helicopter, but then you would miss a great media story and photo opportunity. Never let a good crisis go to waste.

9. B) You must project strength as a dictator. If your citizens are obese or starving you will incur significant healthcare costs and project weakness to the world. Encouraging citizens to plant fruit trees in urban areas will provide a long term, sustainable and economical solution to good health. Banning bacon is likely to incite violence. Your citizens love their bacon.

10. D) One of the most effective ways to undermine another nation is by destroying their currency. By forcing Oilland to conduct commerce in Bestland's currency, you greatly

reduce the power of their local government. In addition to attacking their currency a real war may be helpful. But in this day and age unprovoked wars are looked down upon. Therefore you should call this attack a "humanitarian mission". This situation may be intense, so the best way to lighten-up things is by getting a new puppy.

CHAPTER 5:

WORLD DOMINATION

You are now a political prodigy. You have beaten ineffective politicians at their own game, by mastering the illusion of power. You have given your citizens real hope, by solving fake problems and glossing over real ones. You have given them patriotism and purpose, with humanitarian wars and irrational mega projects. Now it's time to grace more territories with your righteousness.

Billions of people throughout the world are censored by oppressive regimes. They are silently calling for you to free them. Now go forth and liberate them from corrupt governments. Topple all the evil regimes of the world and replace them with yours. Simplify the world map, so that it reads the name of just one nation – your nation. Don't do it for the romantic affairs, movie rights, spoils of war, or any rational reason. Conquer all the nations of the world, so that the children of posterity may live in peace and harmony.

AFTERWORD

I wrote this book to vent my political frustrations. I hope you found it both thought provoking and humorous.

If you enjoyed it, please recommend it to three friends or write a review on Amazon.com. If you disliked it, then please recommend it to three of your greatest enemies.

Feel free to contact me at MattByron.com.

Best Wishes,

Matt Byron